RINGLING BROTHERS
AND
BARNUM & BAILEY
COMBINED
CIRCUS

BOSTOCK'S GREAT ANIMAL ARENA
THE SACRED TATTOOED BULL
FROM THE TEMPLE OF BUDDHA BENARES
THE ONLY ONE EVER ALLOWED BY THE
HIGH PRIEST OF BUDDHA TO LEAVE THE TEMPLE
DREAMLAND CONEY ISLAND

# STEP RIGHT THIS WAY

# STEP RIGHT THIS WAY

## THE PHOTOGRAPHS OF EDWARD J. KELTY

**MILES BARTH     ALAN SIEGEL**

**ESSAY BY EDWARD HOAGLAND**

BARNES
&NOBLE
BOOKS
NEW YORK

2002 Barnes & Noble Books

©2002 by Michael Friedman Publishing Group, Inc.

Library of Congress Cataloging-in-Publication Data available upon request.

ISBN 0-7607-3784-3

Preface by Alan Siegel © 2002
Introduction by Miles Barth © 2002
"The Magic Cavalcade" by Edward Hoagland © 2001

Edited by Miles Barth and Alan Siegel
Project Editor: Betsy Beier
Art Director: Jeff Batzli
Production Manager: Richela Fabian Morgan

Designed by Bethany Johns
Color separations by Chrome Graphics (Overseas) PTE LTD
Printed in Singapore by CS Graphics PTE LTD

10 9 8 7 6 5 4 3 2 1

Visit our website:
www.bn.com

endpapers: Head shots, Ringling Brothers and Barnum & Bailey Circus, Madison Square Garden, 1929 (detail) (front); Head shots, Sells-Floto Circus, Bridgeport, Connecticut, 1932 (back)

page 2: Edward J. Kelty and his banquet camera, c. 1932 (Photographer unknown)

opposite: Bostock's Great Animal Arena, Dreamland, Coney Island, c. 1907

pages 6–7: Ringling Brothers and Barnum & Bailey Circus clowns assembled behind Madison Square Garden, c. 1931 (cyanotype)

# CONTENTS

CONGRESS of FREAKS with RINGLING BROTHERS and BARNUM & BAILEY (COMBINED) CIRCUS SEASON - 1929

# PREFACE

BY ALAN SIEGEL

*Step Right This Way* is a long-overdue tribute to Edward J. Kelty for his extraordinary photographs documenting the American traveling circuses of the 1920s and 1930s. The idea for its publication began to germinate shortly after I bought my first Kelty photograph, *Congress of Freaks with Ringling Brothers and Barnum & Bailey Circus*, at a Sotheby's auction in 1975. I was so taken with this image that I displayed it in my living room alongside prints by Irving Penn, Robert Frank, Diane Arbus, Lisette Model, and Weegee (Arthur Fellig). My family and friends were drawn immediately to this Felliniesque image. Kelty's work was viewed as art, on a par with some of the greatest modern photographers.

After that first purchase, I sent the word out to the photographic community that I wanted to see more of Kelty's work. Photographs began to trickle in, but most of the prints were made seventy or eighty years ago and were in various stages of disintegration. It was extremely frustrating to see fabulous photographs of the opening night at the Barnum & Bailey Circus at Madison Square Garden now turned brownish-yellow with age, their marvelous details faded beyond recognition. It took another two years of tireless research by Miles Barth to uncover biographical information on the enigmatic Kelty and to locate the rich body of prints, acquired and treasured by a handful of circus collectors and museums, that we would use for this book and an accompanying exhibit at the International Center of Photography.

opposite: Congress of Freaks at Ringling Brothers and Barnum & Bailey Circus, Madison Square Garden, 1929 (detail)

I asked Edward Hoagland to write a personal essay for the book after I read his article "Calliope Times" in *The New Yorker*, in which he recounts his experience traveling with the Ringling Brothers and Barnum & Bailey Circus in the summers of 1951 and 1952, during his breaks from classes at Harvard. If you want to learn more about the golden age of the traveling circus as viewed by Mr. Hoagland, you will enjoy his exuberant first novel, *Cat Man*, and chapter three of his latest work, *Compass Points*, describing the seedy, sweaty side of circus life.

Miles Barth and I would like to thank the following individuals for their assistance, generosity, and hospitality: Howard C. Tibbals, the premier model-circus builder in this country and one of the great collectors of circus memorabilia, who provided invaluable background on the rich history of the circus and greatly assisted in every way possible; Fred Dahlinger, the Curator of Collections, and Erin Foley, Archivist, from the Robert L. Parkinson Library and Research Center at the Circus World Museum in Baraboo, Wisconsin, who were especially helpful in supplying historical names, dates, images, and other materials from their collections; and Fred D. Pfening, Jr., the editor of *Bandwagon*, and Fred D. Phening, III, his son and former president of the Circus Historical Society, who shared their wonderful collections and astonishing knowledge of circus history. As Kelty was drawn to sideshows, so was Ken Harck, who has one of the premier collections of relics from Coney, and has lent generously to this volume.

For additional help with research on the book, we would also like to thank Craig Williams, senior historian at the New York State Museum; Kathi Doak at Time, Inc.; Andrew Eskind and Todd Gustavson at the International Museum

of Photography at George Eastman House; and Harold Barnes for his important and wonderful correspondence.

Our thanks also to Linda Raskin of Siegelgale, who masterfully edited the texts and gave numerous suggestions for their improvement, and to the staff at Friedman/Fairfax, who are true professionals and a pleasure to collaborate with.

I invite you to take out your magnifying glasses to fully appreciate the magnificent faces, costumes, and circus graphics depicted in the incomparable photographs of Edward J. Kelty.

ALAN SIEGEL
*May 2002*
*New York City*

Clyde Beatty–Cole Bros. Circus,
New York Hippodrome, New York City, 1937 (detail)

# EDWARD J. KELTY

BY MILES BARTH

## AND CENTURY FLASHLIGHT PHOTOGRAPHERS

Ed Kelty, photographer, takes a picture.

WHEN WORLD WAR I ENDED in late 1918, thousands of American servicemen returned home to continue their lives, or start new ones. Among them was thirty-year-old Edward J. Kelty, whose military induction papers from the Navy in 1917 listed his profession as a reporter and photographer for *The San Francisco Examiner*. Upon his discharge from military service, Kelty took up residence in New York City, where he began assisting several commercial photographers in studio, location, and darkroom work. Kelty learned to use large-format cameras while working at the Byron Company, and it was there that he also developed a keen sense of the photography business. In February 1922, after just two years of apprenticing as a photographer's assistant, Kelty opened his first studio, Century Flashlight Photographers, Inc. The term "flashlight" was photographic jargon that came from the use of powdered magnesium as a flash powder to illuminate dark or indoor locations when making exposures.

Kelty's first studio was located at 120 West Forty-fourth Street in Manhattan, between Fifth and Sixth Avenues. This midtown location was crucial for Kelty's business, since he specialized in photographing weddings, corporate events, and organizational gatherings, most of which took place in the ballrooms of various midtown hotels and the private rooms of restaurants. Kelty also documented the interiors of offices, factories, and commercial buildings, rendering them in extraordinary detail. On the back of his early prints he stamped "Pictures of Special Events Taken in Hotels, Your Home, Office or Factory, Day & Night Service."

During the mid-1920s, many photographers were changing from the bulky and heavy tripod-mounted cameras with glass plates to newer, more portable, hand-held box cameras that used improved lenses and faster films. Kelty continued to use large-format cameras. Two of these, standard eight-by-ten-inch

opposite: Edward Kelty photographing a "congress" of clowns, c. 1934 (photograph by Eddie Jackson)

(20 x 25cm) and eleven-by-fourteen-inch (28 x 36cm) cameras, were employed for portraits, small-group photos, or architectural images. But it was his mammoth, custom-built banquet camera, with negatives up to twelve-by-twenty inches (30 x 51cm), that created Kelty's most dramatic, striking, and memorable images. This banquet camera weighed almost twenty-five pounds (11kg), and depending on the lens he needed for a particular situation, could become even heavier. Often, in order to accommodate the scale of his subject, he would have to raise his tripod more than five feet (2m); with particularly large groups, he would place both camera and tripod on the roof of his truck or mount them on a tall ladder. Under his dark cloth, used to eliminate ambient light and allow him to focus the image, Kelty viewed his subject upside-down and backwards on the ground glass, a characteristic of lens optics that made it difficult for him to anticipate just how well the photograph would turn out until he developed it in the darkroom.

In the summer of 1921, Kelty became drawn to the circus sideshows of Coney Island. The subway had been extended to this seaside resort a year earlier, and now, for a five-cent ride, millions could throng the beach, board-walk, and amusement parks, visit the dance halls, beer gardens, and restaurants, or enjoy the Dixie Reviews with their Minstrel Shows and nightly Charleston contests. The sideshows at Coney Island attracted thousands of people each day, who paid ten cents to gawk at a parade of midgets, giants and giantesses, strongmen and bearded ladies, fat men and women, sword swallowers, fire eaters, alligator men, and tattooed women. The featured acts were the big draw. Barkers shouting "Step right this way" through megaphones enticed crowds to behold such headliners as Bobby the Bulldog Girl; Grady Styles, the Lobster Boy; The Carlson Sisters, Wrestling Fat Girls; Jean Eugene, Half-Woman, Half-Man; Norma, the Four-Legged Girl; Josepha, the Double-Bodied

Girl; and Jolly Irene, America's Largest Girl, Weighing 603 Pounds. Many of the proprietors of the sideshows and circuses at Coney Island (and later on 42nd Street and Palisades Park in New Jersey) hired Kelty to make publicity photographs of their performers and show fronts for use in advertising and sales to the public. He would also take group photographs at their dinners and association conventions.

Kelty's affinity for the human oddities, novelty acts, menageries, and other unusual attractions at Coney Island whetted his passion for circus life. Thus it was a natural progression for Kelty to expand his photographic pursuit from documenting the attractions of Coney Island to photographing the circuses themselves. A year after his first visit to Coney Island, in the summer of 1922, Kelty loaded his cameras into a small truck he had outfitted with enough space to sleep, develop his negatives, and make contact prints, and left the city to follow the circuses that performed up and down the East Coast. At first he focused on the circuses in New York, New Jersey, and Connecticut, but by the late 1920s he was covering circuses throughout the Northeast. In the 1930s Kelty expanded his travels to include various cities in the Midwest, West, and eventually the Northwest. He photographed all the large train shows, including Ringling Brothers and Barnum & Bailey, Cole Brothers, Hagenbeck-Wallace, Sells-Floto, John Robinson Circus, and Al G. Barnes, as well as the smaller wagon and truck shows, such as Hunt's Circus, Sam B. Dill's Circus, and the Silvan-Drew Motorized Circus.

Edward Kelty was the Cecil B. DeMille of still photography, assembling and directing large groups of circus performers and staff, in some cases more than a thousand people, to pose for the spectacular images that showcased the

MRS. JIMMIE FOSTER

FLINT MICH

JULY 5, 1932.

DON SMITH—JIMMIE FOSTER— ED KELTY

Kelty (right) poses with circus and Wild West show performers Mr. and Mrs. Jimmie Foster (center and on horseback) and Circus Historical Society founder Don Smith (left) in Flint, Michigan, July 5, 1932. (Photographer unknown)

Front cover of Kelty's 1929
sales catalogue

diversity and oddity of this unique way of life. Although best known in the circus community for these monumental undertakings, Kelty also took portraits of individual performers, landscapes of circus lots, and interiors of the big tops. His photographic routine at the circus rarely changed. The demanding schedule would begin at dawn, when he set up his tripods and cameras so he could start shooting right after breakfast. The groups to be photographed were chosen based on their availability; the performers usually posed last because of their extensive preparations with costumes and makeup. By noon he would have made as many as thirty negatives, approximately three to four alternative shots for each group. He would spend the afternoon processing the film and making sample prints, which he showed to the performers, circus management, and roustabouts before the evening performance. After taking their orders, Kelty would return to his truck, where he printed late into the evening so that the finished prints would be ready for distribution before the circus left town for their next venue. Kelty rarely spent more than a day or two at each circus, unless he was traveling beyond New York or New Jersey, so that he could return to his studio to service his wedding and banquet business.

Kelty rarely photographed circus rehearsals or actual performances: this was left to another major circus photographer, Harry Atwell, of Chicago. For almost twenty years, the careers of Kelty and Atwell followed similar trajectories, but with a few significant differences. Atwell focused almost exclusively on candid, documentary shots, using a hand-held box camera to give him the mobility to capture the spontaneous events that took place before and during the performances. He also had a studio where he made more intimate portraits that were distributed to the press. Kelty, with his massive banquet camera, tripod, and slow film, specialized in more controlled, formal images. As an employee of Ringling Brothers and Barnum & Bailey, Atwell had complete

and unrestricted access, while Kelty, an independent contractor, was forced to give 50 percent of his revenues to the circus's management in exchange for their cooperation in making their employees available to him.

Starting in 1925, Kelty published modest non-illustrated sales catalogues to promote his circus and sideshow photographs. These brochures were divided into "Circus Pictures" and "Side Show Pictures" and further broken down by the particular year, or "season." The last section of his brochure featured his "Unusual Pictures." Kelty has the distinction of being the first photographer to make flash photographs in Madison Square Garden, and his 1929 brochure mentioned many of these images, including *Aboriginal Council-Indian Group*, *6 Days Bicycle Race*, *Checho-Slovakian Band*, *Entrants in America's Venus Contest*, *Entrants in America's Apollo Contest*, *Marathon Dance (Taken at end of 361 Hours and 45 Minutes of Continuous Dancing)*, *National Association of Amusement Park Directors*, *C.C. Pyles' Coast to Coast Runners*, and *The Great Wilno*. Kelty made most of his money selling prints to the employees of the circus; he also licensed his pictures to entertainment trade publications like *The Billboard*, *Variety*, *The White Tops* (the official journal of the Circus Fans Association of America), and to the members of other circus-related organizations.

The Depression took a terrible toll on the circus and on Kelty. In 1929 there were thirteen railroad shows touring the United States; by the 1933 season, only three of the railroad shows remained in operation. Many of the smaller shows closed during the season, leaving performers, staff, and animals stranded in small towns across the country. Some shows were so hard hit they never left their winter quarters. Others that were not shut down were purchased by the larger, more established enterprises and often combined with existing shows such as Ringling Brothers and Barnum & Bailey.

Inside page of Kelty's 1929
sales catalogue

Kelty's hotel and corporate photography business also suffered from the weakened economy. His clients had few reasons to celebrate in this climate. With his commercial business on the decline, Kelty intensified his photographic work with the circus. In 1935, according to his brochure, more than fifty new images were added for sale. The advertisement in this brochure read: "ALL PICTURES—12 x 20 inches—$1.25 for singles—6 for $6.00—12 for $10.00." At this time his studio was located at 110 West Forty-sixth Street, and his stationery read "Edward J. Kelty—Winter Quarters—Century Photographers." At some point between 1938 and the early 1940s, still struggling to make ends meet, Kelty was forced to sell a significant number of his negatives to Knickerbocker Photos, a company that distributed photographic images to magazines, periodicals, and textbook publishers. With offices in Manhattan and Brooklyn, Knickerbocker sold Kelty's circus prints to a broader audience than he could do on his own.

Kelty was an enigmatic figure. Born in Denver in 1888, he served as Ship's Cook Third Class in the Navy during World War I. In February 1926, he married Annette Peterson, who worked for him as a secretary in his studio. The Keltys separated shortly before the birth of their second son, and both boys grew up knowing little about their father. Around 1942, Kelty made his last circus photographs and moved to Chicago. Although there is little record of his life in Chicago, it is known that he worked for a time as a vendor at Wrigley Field and was a member of organizations such as the American Legion and the Old Timers' Baseball Association. At his death in 1967, there was little evidence of his career in photography: a few albums of photos taken in the Navy and a handful of circus prints, found in his small Chicago apartment.

Few original Kelty negatives remain in existence. The vast majority were produced on nitrate-based film, an unstable medium that inevitably caused the emulsion carrying the image to disintegrate. It is rumored that he donated his eight-by-ten-inch (20 x 25cm) and eleven-by-fourteen-inch (28 x 36cm) negatives to a World War II scrap drive. One story related by several collectors is that Kelty often hocked his negatives to settle his bar bills at several midtown saloons, which they failed to return in the same condition or number that he had deposited. According to the story, several hundred of his negatives were later found in the storeroom of a bar and sold to a circus memorabilia collector in Florida, but have since disintegrated. What is left of Kelty's work today are his photographic prints, largely relegated to a few circus memorabilia collectors or circus and entertainment history collections.

During the twenty years he followed the circuses, Edward J. Kelty created photographs that captured the spirit and atmosphere of the big top better than any other photographer. Rarely retouched or cropped, they are pure evidence of those who stood in front of his massive cameras. His is a body of work that will remain forever unique in the annals of circus history, a fascinating visual record of one of America's favorite forms of entertainment. As we view these images today, we are reminded of our school class photos: standing on the bleachers, facing the camera, holding still. We can imagine ourselves as the clowns, aerialists, acrobats, animal trainers and handlers, ticket takers, musicians, equestrians, or any of the other participants in the circus, taking our cues from this quintessential ringmaster. These images provide us with a legacy of an era that we will remember in the same light as the historic circus parades—gone, but fortunately not forgotten.

Edward Kelty flanked by members of the Hagenbeck-Wallace Circus, c. 1935 (Photographer unknown)

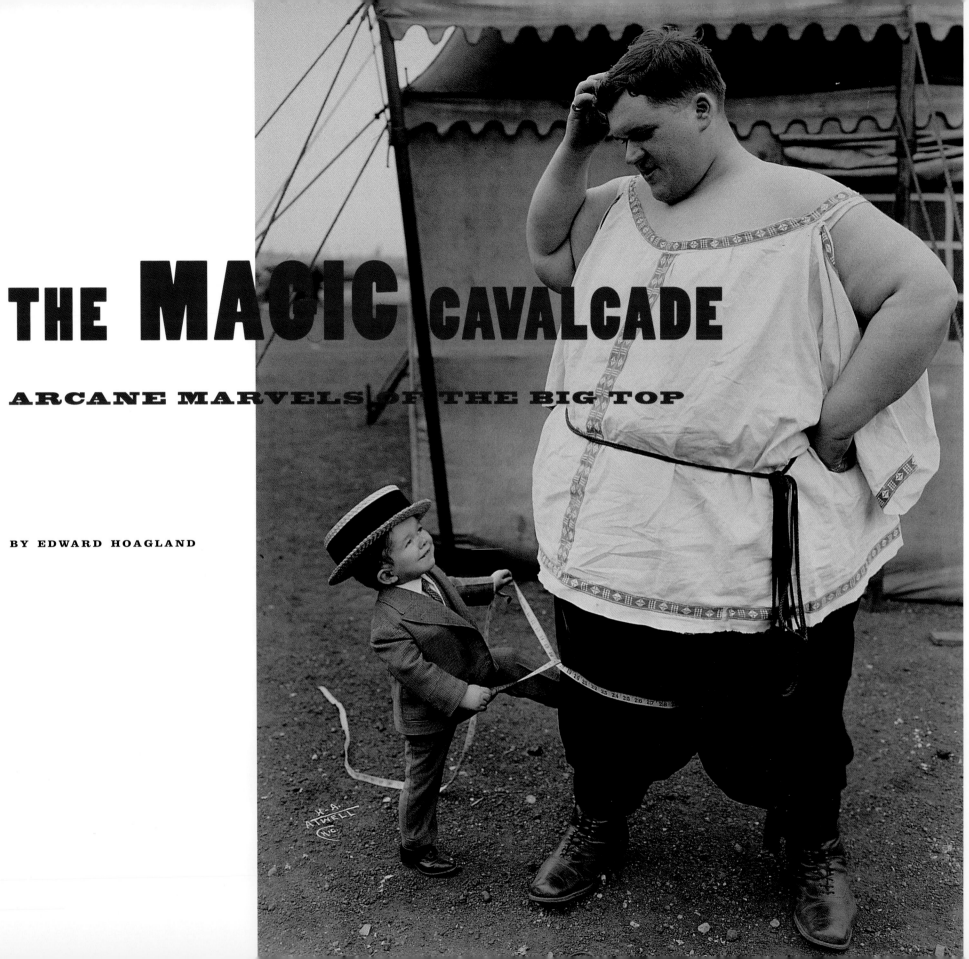

# THE MAGIC CAVALCADE

## ARCANE MARVELS OF THE BIG TOP

BY EDWARD HOAGLAND

A CIRCUS IS both acrobatic and elephantine, wholesome but freakish, and that is partly why we like it so—because we are two-headed, too. A showgirl in the center ring displays her pretty legs to daddy, while his children are engrossed in watching her palomino stallion dance to the band's tempo. It's an illusion, of course. The bandmaster, flourishing his silver cornet, is actually following the horse's mannered, jerky prance, not vice-versa, which in turn is being cued by the same short-skirted lady's cracking whip.

In the old days, circus sideshows used to be called "The Ten-In-One" because they had, as the barkers yelled, "Ten Different Freaks Under One Tent for Only One Dollar! Can you beat that, folks?" Only, I suppose, by looking inside oneself.

*"We have the fattest women in the world, and the tallest man, and a girl who has no arms or legs, and midgets who are married! Have you ever seen a camel spit, or seals play catch, or elephants stand on their heads? A man with reptile scales who was once just like you! And the Good Lord made him. Can you finish your ice cream after you have looked at him?"*

Good question. In the pre-television era, when much of the novel technology related to transportation, not electronics, live entertainment toured between cities by train or motor vehicle. Repertory stage and opera companies, evangelist preachers, Chautauqua lecturers, freelance physic salesmen, vaudeville magicians, humorists, and strippers, who formerly had gone by riverboat or wagon, would troop through town—as would the more celebrated Sells-Floto, or Sparks, or Hagenbeck-Wallace, or Sam B. Dill's, or Water L. Main, or Robbins Bros., and Christy Bros. circuses, not to mention

"We have the fattest women in the world, and the tallest man, and a girl who has no arms or legs, and midgets who are married! Have you ever seen a camel spit, or seals play catch, or elephants stand on their heads?"

opposite: Major Mite and Tom Ton, c. 1925 (Photograph by Harry Atwell Studio)

Maybe the grisly part of the bargain is that we, the "lot lice," the "Elmers," rubes, towners, hayseeds, hicks, yokels, are paying green money to watch the star troupers risk their lives.

Ringling Bros. and Barnum & Bailey, The Greatest Show on Earth. There was Downie Bros. Wild Animal Circus, The Largest Motor Circus in the World (families and brothers stuck together in those days), and the famous Clyde Beatty–Cole Brothers big show, and W.P. Johnson's World Champion Cowgirls, and Col. Tim McCoy & His Indian Line Up, or his Congress of the World's Rough Riders, and Marcellus' Golden Models (with the men's pectorals as big as the women's breasts), and Tommy Atkins' Military Riding Maids.

In the big top everybody wears a spiffy uniform, but if your circus isn't a one-night stand and it stays until tomorrow, you'll see some of the circus people sleeping in the horse straw on the ground. And when the costumes come off, baby, don't imagine they'll remember you, no matter how hard you clapped. Behind the greasepaint is quite a different sort of face and person. You wouldn't necessarily trust one of the clowns or animal handlers who give such intense pleasure to tens of thousands of children with the downright raising of even one or two; they might already have abandoned a family. Like actors, only more so, circus performers are expected to be manic and depressive, and we accept the paradox that a real genius at making little kids laugh, like a Danny Kaye or a Charlie Chaplin, could also verge on frightening them as a father.

A circus is high and low, trombones and piccolos. The edgy tiger roars and charges, but then licks her trainer at the end, as if they had been friends all along. A clown meanly tricks his chum, dunks him treacherously in a barrel of water, and gloats for the crowd, teaching us most memorably that if you trust

anybody, he will betray you. Then the high-wire walker steals all his thunder
as soon as the whistle blows. The ringmaster, though he seems to be the boss,
is curiously not the star; the saddest puss gets the biggest laugh and the inno-
cence is raunchy (those leggy girls who strut their stuff alongside a whiteface
Bozo). The funniness is vertiginous and the hippodrome food is too sweet.
Too much is going on in the rings to absorb it all. Physical stunts sometimes
edge toward the suicidal. Maybe the grisly part of the bargain is that we, the
"lot lice," the "Elmers," rubes, towners, hayseeds, hicks, yokels, are paying
green money to watch the star troupers risk their lives. If a trapeze artist falls
and hits the ground, he'll lie in front of a grandstand of utter strangers,
whimpering, jactitating, and dying alone.

We want circus people to be different from us—homeless and garish,
heedless and tawdry (otherwise, why pay to watch?)—yet to connect with us in
deeper currents that we share: our fear of heights and ridicule, our complicated
fascination with animals (whips, but kindness), our love of grace and agility, of

opposite: Cole Brothers
Circus poster, 1935

above: Ringling Brothers
and Barnum & Bailey Circus
posters from 1929 (left) and
1938 (right)

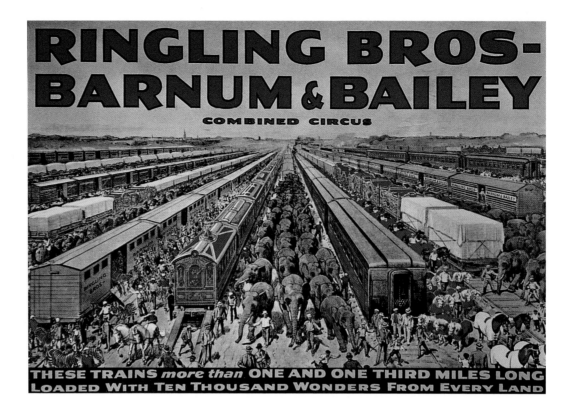

stylish vanity and splendid boasting, of dressing in spangles while living in tents and trailers. We want the showpeople to be outlandish but never outrageous, to hide from us their perverse, larcenous, or alcoholic tendencies that may accompany the tramping life. A guy who just got out of the county jail (we hope not the Big House) for doing whatever (and we don't want to know the whatever) and then hit the road because his wife didn't want him is coiling and flinging the ropes that keep the aerialists' rigging up; somehow it has become the kind of responsibility he can handle.

As an element of rooting our children in a stable home, we nourish them with this annual spectacle of the elaborately raffish and picaresque. Without quite articulating it, we want our offspring to be flexible and adventurous as well as predictable, tolerant as well as ethical, capable of flights of delight as well as down to earth. Also, we want circus people to know us better than we know them, in a sense: to be wise beyond what their education and social status should officially warrant in gauging human nature, to cater to and inspire our children, even though we have come to watch some of them risk breaking their necks—which is base of us—and even if they can't always manage their own private behavior. Circus people are juggling themselves—hand-to-mouth, in brassy penury—not just tossing torches or chancing an awful clawing. They'll live in backstreet rented rooms in the winter until they can take to the road again.

It's no coincidence that circus music is identical to the marches that soldiers used to go off to die to. The stakes are high. Bravery, resourcefulness, pinpoint concentration, and self-containment are what make it work. One reason so many losers have found their footing in the circus may be because they see in the crowds how thin a veneer conventional society paints upon our basic greed, inertia, and callousness. So why worry that you're an oddball and have to sublimate your haywire impulses in stunts, or move somewhere new every other day to keep them under control? Like the rich, circus people have that privilege. New audience, new town, never seen you before, never see you again. It's anesthetic. If you screw up one of the acts today, you'll get it right tomorrow—so, no sweat, you get it right today.

FORTUNATELY, WE AREN'T ENTIRELY BEREFT of a visual record of these arcane marvels. A Manhattan banquet photographer named Edward J. Kelty, whose usual venue was hotel ballrooms and Christmas parties, went out intermittently in the summers, from the early 1920s to the early 1940s, to take wide-angle, tripod pictures of circus personnel in what could only have constituted a labor of love. His bread-and-butter job already made him an expert at joshing smiles and camaraderie out of disparate collections of people, coaxing them to

It's no coincidence that circus music is identical to the marches that soldiers used to go off to die to.

drape their arms around each other and trust the box's eye. He would pose an ensemble of horse wranglers, cavemen, ticket takers, candy butchers, teeterboard tumblers, "web-sitters" (guys who hold the ropes for the aerial ballet girls), and limelight daredevils, or the bosses and moneymen. He photographed everybody, roustabouts as conscientiously as impresarios, and although he was not artistically very ambitious—he would hawk his prints to the troupers at "6 for $5"—he surely aspired, in his consuming hobby, to document this vivid, disreputable demimonde obsessively and thoroughly. This is his gift to us.

His subjects may have been more camera-shy than publicity hounds, but Kelty's rubber-chicken award ceremonies and industrial photo shoots must have taught him how to relax jumpy people for the few minutes required to capture the shot. With his Broadway pinstripes and his newsman's bent fedora, he must have become a trusted presence in the "Backyard" and "Clown Alley." He knew the show business and street touts, bookies and scalpers. He knew how to let the sangfroid sing from some of these faces (or simply the good rolling-stone mischief), while doing justice to the ragged string beans ranked in a line. These tribes of showboaters must have amused him after the winter-time's chore of recording for posterity some forty-year drudge receiving a gold watch.

Other faces seem muddied with inchoate emotions, however, as if they had indeed just gotten out of the penitentiary, or were mentally retarded, or could already feel the dreadful undertow of an illness like epilepsy, schizophrenia, pedophilia, kleptomania, tuberculosis, or diabetic collapse that had choked off so many fresh starts that he had attempted before. You wouldn't see faces like these in one of Kelty's hotel ballroom shots, even on the waiters.

Kelty's images telegraph the complexity of the circus hierarchy: the ushers, the prop men and riggers, the cookhouse crew, the elephant men and cat men, the showgirls arrayed in white bathing suits in a tightly chaperoned, winsome line, the hoboes who had put the tent up and in the wee hours would tear it down, and the bosses with arms akimbo and swaggering legs—all tell us something of who they were. Stars at the top, winos at the bottom. Except that still below the winos were the "jigs," or Negroes, whom you may notice in uneasily angular positions as they perch semi-perilously on a wagon roof behind everyone else, up in "nigger heaven" (as expressed in moviehouse terms) signifying their loose-balloon moorings in this segregated world, based

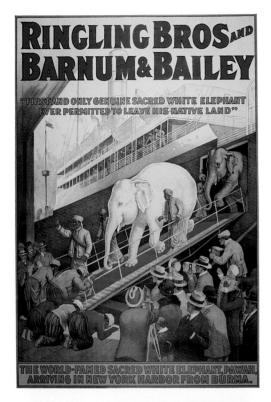

on the mores of winter quarters, which was usually down South. There may even be two bands in the picture, a black one and a white one, which might have sounded better playing together.

During long winter months, arranging corporate personnel in the phony bonhomie of an office get-together for a company's annual report, Kelty must have longed for summer, when he would be snapping "Congresses" of mugging clowns, fugueing freaks, rodeo sharpshooters, plus the train crews known as "razorbacks" (*Raise your backs!*), who loaded and unloaded the wagons from railroad flatcars at midnight and dawn. These ladies toted pythons as they strolled around the hippodrome track, and didn't wear enough clothes; some of the guys looked as bathless as the guys from a hobo jungle who steal your wife's pie that she'd left to cool on the kitchen windowsill, yet had skills you hadn't imagined. Circuses flouted convention as part of their pitch—flaunted and cashed in on the romance of outlawry, like Old World gypsies. If there wasn't a crime wave when the show was in town, everybody sure expected one. And the exotic physiognomies, strangely cut clothes, and oddly focused, disciplined bodies were almost as disturbing: "Near Eastern," whatever Near Eastern meant (it somehow sounded weirder than "Middle Eastern," or "Far Eastern"), Bedouin Arabs, Turks and Persians, or Pygmies, Zulus, people cicatrized, "platter-lipped," or nose-split. That was the point. They came from all over the known world to parade down Main Street on gaudy, ten-hitch wagons or caparisoned elephants, and then, like the animals in the cages, you wanted them to leave town. Yet if you were a farmer who thought that a bear that had killed a pig was scary to come to grips with, try managing half a dozen snarling lions! Or maybe you had screwed up your nerve recently to reroof the barn? Try walking the high wire, fifty feet up, with just your wife standing underneath you in case of a slip.

top: Ringling Brothers and Barnum & Bailey Circus poster, 1927

bottom: Hagenbeck-Wallace Circus poster, 1938

CIRCUS DAY WAS UNCIVILIZED like the Fourth of July, with candied apples, cotton candy, fireworks, and special dispensation for skimpy costumes, public lust, trials of strength, breakneck stunts, and colossal crowds. "It was a circus," we'll still say when some ordinary scene bursts out of control. And if your blouse stuck out farther that the next girl's, that cage boy loafing over there might decide to persuade the hippopotamus to gape her mouth for you and poke his hand inside and scratch her gums the way she liked, to make you ooh and aah at how heroic he was.

I was such a cage boy myself, with Ringling Bros. and Barnum & Bailey in 1951 and 1952, and would also pet the menagerie leopards for the right admirer. The men in these pictures remind me of the men I worked with for two dollars per sixteen-hour day (doubtless twice what Kelty's workhands earned twenty years earlier)—and in fact slept with, because we were required to sleep two-to-a-bunk, three bunks high, on the train, or else we could rattle through the night outside on a flatcar.

The faces of the drifters in the Sells-Floto montage can look as grim and bitter as a Wanted poster, and quite at their wit's end, not having had much wit to begin with and what they might have had perhaps dispelled in prison. They've slammed around, with their hats pulled down over their eyes, every mother-in-law's nightmare, and know how to jump on a moving train without saying goodbye to anybody—know the Front Range of the Rockies and the Tex-Mex border. And not even Kelty, our rumpled banquets guy with the windblown tie, a theater-district barfly and Coney Island dime museum habitué, could coax a trustful look out of them.

Up on that giddy wire or the trapeze bar—or in the Iron Jaw act, spinning relentlessly by their teeth—people did things they shouldn't reasonably do, with no ostensible purpose but to show off, while the tuba oomphed, the trombone

They came from all over the known world to parade down Main Street on gaudy, ten-hitch wagons or caparisoned elephants

"Is your body as trim as mine?" they seem to ask. "I'll stand on one hand —or one finger!"

slalomed, the clarinet climbed a rope, and the cornet hit the canvas's peak line. "Flyers" and slack-wire artists and "risley" foot-jugglers and whiteface or "auguste" clowns hoarded and pruned their skills—like the humble juggler of legend, who during the night tiptoed into the empty cathedral on the Madonna's feast day after the wealthier citizens had long since delivered their heavy gifts, genuflected before her statue, and went comfortably home. Alone and barefoot, the juggler performed for her with whatever grace and dexterity he could muster. And for the first time in history, tears welled in her stone eyes.

That's what we all try to do, isn't it? Keep rolling, keep juggling and strutting our stuff, honoring our gods; then take a bow and exit smiling? But magic seldom happens unless a structure has been erected—whether a church or a tent—that is hospitable to it. Art is fragile, and windless silence helps. Then depart just as the applause crests, leaving some emotion for the next act, because the thrust of a circus never stops, whether in mud or sunshine, whether the tickets have sold out or not. High stakes.

The aerialist Lillian Leitzel, the most mesmerizing female performer ever, fell to her death in 1931, and afterwards Alfred Codona, her husband and male counterpart at least on the trapeze, married an equestrienne but injured himself while doing a triple somersault in 1933 and never flew again. Grotesquely, he became his wife's hostler, until, estranged, he shot both her and himself in her divorce lawyer's office. More recently, Karl Wallenda, the greatest wirewalker and another compulsive, fell twelve stories off a cable strung between two hotels, at age seventy-three. But for some of these plain old Okies and Arkies and Hoosiers and Wisconsin Cheeseheads and Georgia Crackers who got the show to run on time and then maybe drove a trailer truck all night, the gamble was compelling, too. Their trajectory ran toward alcohol and the jitters of oblivion, even though they had a seaman's way with ropes.

left: Cole Brothers Circus poster, c. 1935

opposite: Ringling Brothers and Barnum & Bailey Circus posters, 1939 (top) and 1934 (bottom)

Several gaze at Kelty's camera as though reminded of a police-station booking room, whereas the performers pose in a row in profile, with their biceps bulged or ponytails pert. "Is your body as trim as mine?" they seem to ask. "I'll stand on one hand—or one finger! I'll do a back flip from one horse to another and then lie down on the ground and let the elephant put her foot on my nose, but because we're all family, she won't crush it. Instead she'll lift me onto her shoulders and we'll chase that clown until he drops his red bloomers."

The moneymen, gimlet-eyed, with peremptory chests, let their suits, cuff-links, and stickpins, their oxblood shoes and railroadmen's timepieces, speak for them. They owned the tents and trucks and railroad cars, of course, but often the lions, too, despite the trainer's intimacy with them. *He* could be fired and have to pack his kit and never see those particular cats again. Similarly, the acrobats were not terribly suited to busking for spare change on the subway. They needed complicated rigging and a spread of canvas overhead— the whole apparatus—to gather an audience sufficient to justify risking their lives, without being clinically crazy. And a run-of-the mill hobo, who was used to sneaking across the hazardous, lightless bustle of a railroad to boost himself into a moving boxcar without being detected, had probably found a reason for being with Ringling Bros., "the show of shows," called by show people "the Big One." In my time, if he was fired with the dreaded words "No Rehire" scribbled on his pink slip to go into the company's records, it might take the little wind that he had out of his sails. The performances, the crowds and ovations, though not directly for him, had centered and justified his shaky life.

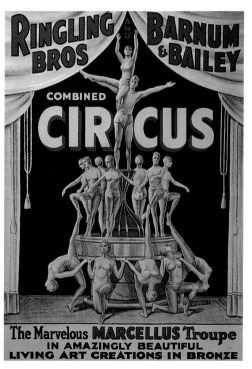

The centerpoles and brocaded, bejeweled elephant howdahs might be bedecked with the Stars and Stripes, and yet—unlike the Fourth of July—

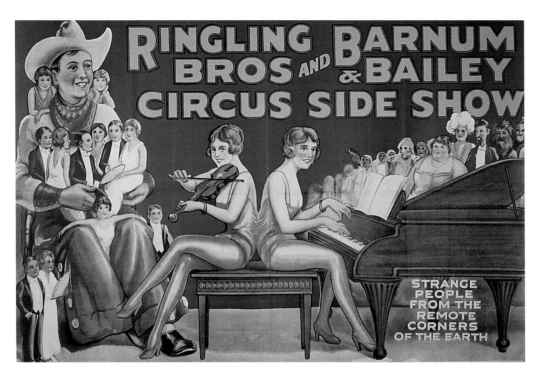

one knew that the entire spectacle wasn't quite *American*. The men and women holding hands in the center ring to take a bow after manipulating their bodies on the teeterboard were probably foreigners and might not even be married to each other, and God knows where they slept. They had gelled their flightiness for professional purposes, but somehow the idea of a new town tomorrow, a new town the next day, and consorting in a business-like way with freaks whose very livelihood was exhibiting their disfigurements like fakirs in an Asian marketplace (freaks were inherently un-American), didn't jibe with the "Home of the Brave." And what demons in themselves were they trying to anesthetize, in harboring values so different from ours? We, the "Elmers," the hicks, the towners, had just put down good money to watch somebody shoot himself out of a cannon on the assurance that it was going to be genuine and that he might really die before our eyes, but he lands succinctly on his back in the L-shaped net, swings to the ground, acknowledges our claps—and doesn't now thank his lucky stars and settle down to a productive existence like ours. *Eat your heart out, Rube,* is part of his message. *We'll be gone tomorrow. We'll see Chicago. We'll be in Florida. You stay here and milk your cows!*

To the "strange people," misshapen on their little stages in the sideshows and peddling ten-cent likenesses of their deformities to the public, the conventional response would be, "There but for the grace of God go I." But why had He withheld His mercy when constructing *them*? Did their burden, as suggested by ancient superstitions, express a spiritual canker? Was external

left: Ringling Brothers and Barnum & Bailey Circus poster, 1935

opposite: Ringling Brothers and Barnum & Bailey Circus poster, 1926–27

ugliness a punishment laid on the erring soul? My own feeling, while working next to them in Madison Square Garden and other arenas half a century ago, was that the object lesson ran deeper still. People were fascinated not just because of morbid curiosity and schadenfreude, but because we saw ourselves incarnate in the Knife-Thrower, the Living Skeleton (or "Pincushion," or "Picture Gallery"), the Human Pretzel, the Fat Lady, the lame and wheezing Giant, and were encouraged to stare without being rude. The foxfire flicker of ferocity and awful insecurity that so frequently

subverted our genial veneer lay out there exposed—much as the bum, the coward, the fussbudget, and the spoilsport whom we knew all too well was embodied in some of the skits the clowns performed. (Our Knife-Thrower really got to people when, as a pièce de résistance, he "horse-whipped" pretty women who volunteered from the crowd.)

A clown or Santa Claus costume, in my experience of the individuals who wear them, can conceal a multitude of sins. But so does the attire that the rest of us hide in, using blandness to mask our shamefaced failures and maladjustments. We, too, have flat feet and big asses, chalky faces and weepy tendencies when frightened of our shadows or when searching through the tanbark for a nickel we have lost, a button that has popped off, or a pebble that was in our shoe (we took it out but now we miss it). In the smaller tent shows, the Fat Lady in the baby-doll nightie might even *show it all* in a curtained-off area if you paid an extra four bits (and it was said you could insert them). In a circus you didn't have to—weren't supposed to—avert your eyes, and that may have been its ultimate kick. The guy might die, but without muttering the piety "Oh, I can't watch," we simply did.

Uzbeks rode on saddled camels. Elephants sashayed. A swaypole acrobat almost seemed to touch the ground on each backswing, then locked his feet and slid down headfirst. A lovely woman with blonde hair hanging to her coccyx adjusted her shoulder straps, kicked off her silver slippers, and gripped a knotted rope to ascend for the Cloud Swing. Over at one side, we might not notice a self-effacing clown—not bizarrely loud now to attempt to attract attention—pulling her up with considerable care, then standing underneath in case of mishap. But if you were observant, you realized there might be some people who had a love life, after all.

The black-maned lion roared with bestial fury yet soon lapsed into contented amiability, as if he might be willing to settle in our burg. And the Albino Girl and Snake Charmer and other troupers were said to have bought cough medicine and underpants and other personal stuff in the local stores. But just when we thought they really liked us and had been converted to our home-sweet-home values, they up and did a disappearing act. Overnight, the magic cavalcade vanished to another state, and another climate.

And Kelty, our Times Square guy with Broadway savoir-faire, reckless himself (apparently bartering his negatives to his barkeep to pay his tab), had earlier been there to record parts of the impromptu tale, more valuably than perhaps he ever knew. He had the gimpy, haywire gene as well—the one that makes you want to hit the road each spring while you last—a hail-fellow who knew that nothing was for keeps. You do your thing, to whatever tattoo of music and battery of lights that are available to you, survive today, and get up on that wire again tomorrow.

Overnight, the magic
cavalcade vanished
to another state,
and another climate.

# THE PHOTOGRAPHS OF
# EDWARD J. KELTY

# CHAPTER I

# THE SIDESHOWS

## OF CONEY ISLAND, 42ND STREET, AND HARLEM

Kelty's later circus photography had its roots

in the local New York sideshows

he photographed in the early 1920s.

opposite: Un-Named, Coney Island, 1930
right: Hubert's Museum, New York City, 1925 (detail)

Wonderland Circus Sideshow, Coney Island, 1929

Dreamland Circus Sideshow, Coney Island, 1927

John R. Agee and his horses, Luna Park, Coney Island, 1927

opposite: Jolly Dixie, The Nat Reiss Shows, 1927, "The Show with a Worthwhile Reputation"

above: Dreamland Circus Side Show, Coney Island, c. 1925; from left are Tom Ton, Jolly Irene, and The Carlson Sisters

A NIGHT IN DIXIE
DIXIE REVUE
SPECIAL TO-NIGHT
CHARLESTON CONTEST
ADMISSION 10¢
ADMISSION 10¢
CENTURY
144 W 46TH ST,
2235
CONEY ISLAND
—1926—

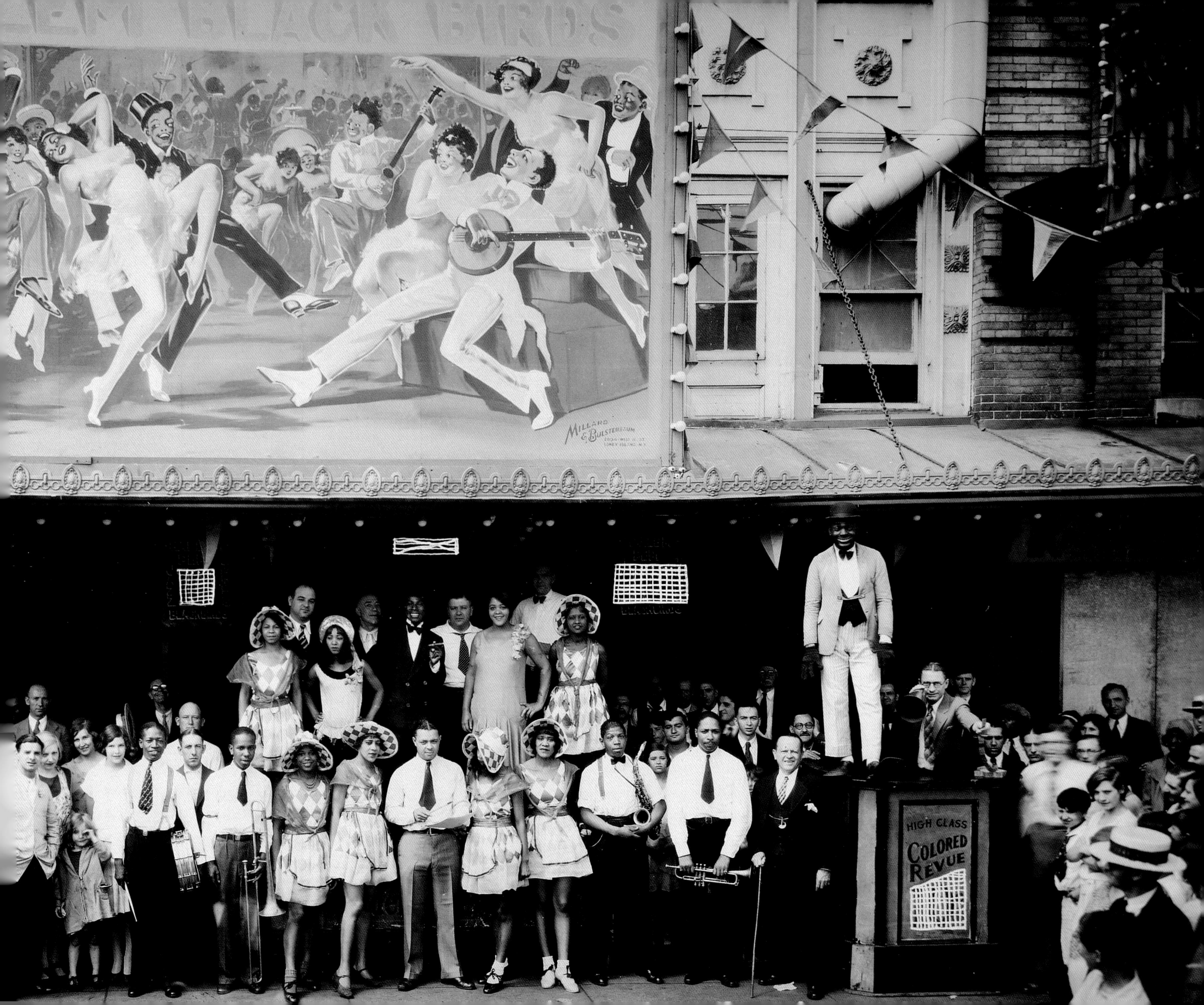
BLACK BIRDS
MILLARD & BULSTERBAUM
HIGH CLASS
COLORED REVUE

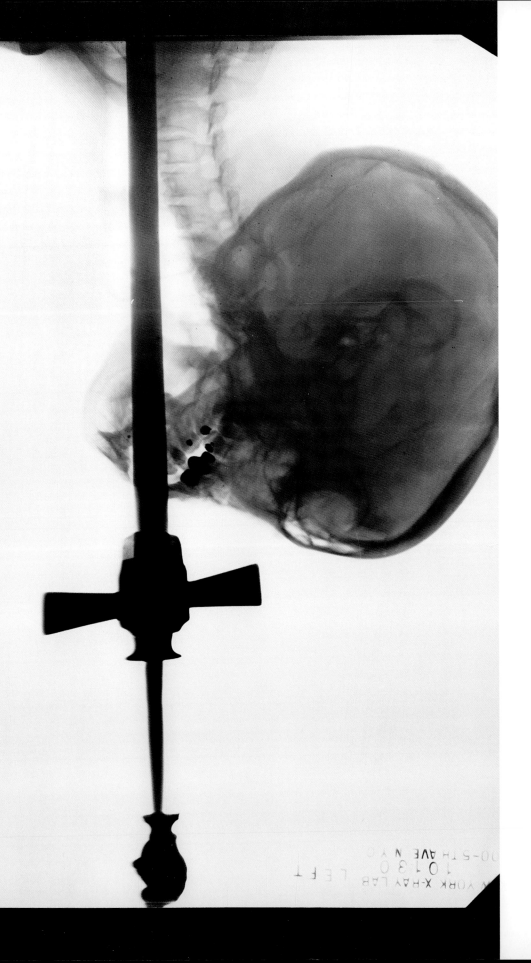

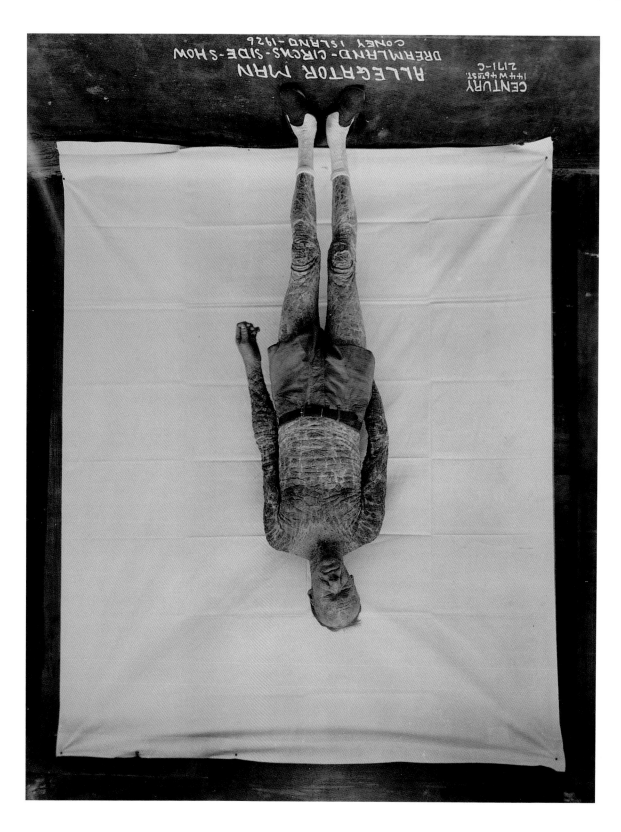

Oriental Village, Luna Park, Coney Island, 1927

Huber's Museum, Coney Island, 1927

above: Hubert's Museum, West Forty-second Street, New York City, 1925
opposite: Harlem Amusement Palace, East 125th Street, New York City, 1924

PLEASE REPORT
ALL COMPLAINTS
AT CASH BOX

HARMONY FIVE
JAZZ QUINTET

HARLEM-AMUSEMENT-PALACE.

150 EAST 125TH STREET          NEW YORK CITY.

DEC. 18TH 1924

CENTURY
105 W 47TH ST.
1115

Temple of Wonders, Palisade Park, New Jersey, 1926

NEW YORK CITY SEPT. 26 1936

U.S.W.P.A. FEDERAL THEATRE CIRCUS UNIT

PHOTO BY E.J. KELTY CENTUR 110 W 46 45-A

## CHAPTER II

# THE SPECTACULAR GROUP SHOTS

These impressive photographic undertakings made Kelty renowned in the world of the circus.

opposite: U.S.W.P.A. Federal Theatre Circus Unit, New York City, 1936
right: Clowns celebrating the "Ringling Golden Jubilee," Brooklyn, 1933 (detail)

PROPERTY OF
TED DE PAOLO
OFFICIAL
MOTION PICTURE
PHOTOGRAPHER
CHARLES SCRIBER SHOWMAN'S CLUB

COLE BROS.—CLYDE BEATTY CIRCUS    NEW YORK HIPP

Clyde Beatty–Cole Bros. Circus, New York Hippodrome, New York City, 1937

Clowns, Hagenbeck-Wallace Circus, Brooklyn, 1931

Sells-Floto Circus, South Ozone Park, New York, 1932

Sideshow band, Ringling Brothers and Barnum & Bailey Circus, c. 1925

Christy Brothers Circus Sideshow, 1933

CONGRESS OF CLOWNS

PHOTO BY
E. J. KELTY
CENTURY
110 W 46 N.Y.C.

PATTERSON, N.J.
JUNE 13, 1935

Congress of Clowns, Ringling Brothers and Barnum & Bailey Circus, Paterson, New Jersey, 1935

Ringling Brothers and Barnum & Bailey Circus clowns assembled behind Madison Square Garden, c. 1931 (cyanotype)

COLE BROTHERS-CLYDE BEATTY CIRCUS

CUMBERLAND, MD.- JULY 27TH 1935

Clyde Beatty–Cole Bros. Circus elephants, Cumberland, Maryland, 1935

Gangler's Novelty Circus, New York, c. 1931

—DOROTHY HERBERT—

RINGLING BROTHERS AND BARNUM & BAILEY COMBINED CIRCUS

Clyde Beatty, Madison Square Garden, 1934

Maxine Penny and Tom Mix, Sells-Floto Circus, Patterson, New Jersey, 1931

Clyde Beatty, Hagenbeck-Wallace Circus, 1931

The Hanneford Troupe, Hagenbeck-Wallace Circus, 1931

Chester E. Barnett and his clown band, Abe Goldstein announcing, Sells-Floto Circus, 1928

The Pina Troupe with V.H. Walker (far left) and
Dorothy Campbell Walker (far right), Christy Bros. Circus, 1929

90

~ THE PINA TROUPE ~
AND
(SLIM)-WALKER AND DOROTHY CAMPBELL WALKER WITH CHRISTY BROS. CIRCUS ~

CENTURY
144 W 46 th ST.
N.Y.C.-1954

LITTLE FALLS, N.Y.
JULY 17, 1935

HAROLD BARNES FEATURED WITH COLE BROTHERS - CLYDE BEATTY

Harold Barnes, Clyde Beatty Cole Bros. Circus, Little Falls, New York, 1935

above and opposite: Knight Troupe, 1930

CENTURY FLASHLIGHT PHOTOGRAPHERS, INC.
70 West 47th St. NEW YORK CITY

RUSH PROOF

CENTURY FLASHLIGHT PHOTOGRAPHERS, INC.
74 WEST 47th ST. NEW YORK CITY

$6 for $5.00 Reorders 50¢ each

—KNIGHT TROUPE—

Dorothy Campbell Walker working Christy Bros. Circus bulls, 1929

—DOROTHY CAMPBELL WALKER—
WORKING
—CHRISTY BROS. CIRCUS BULLS—

PHOTO BY
CENTURY
144 W 46TH ST.
N.Y.C.

The World's Foremost Mid-Air Marvels, Ringling Brothers and Barnum & Bailey Circus, Newark, New Jersey, 1935

Queens of the Air, Ringling Brothers and Barnum & Bailey Circus, Paterson, New Jersey, 1935

Col. W. T. Johnson's World Champion Cowgirls, Madison Square Garden, 1935

COL. W.T. JOHNSON'S WORLD CHAMPION COWGIRLS—MADISON SQUARE GARDEN—NEW YORK CITY—1935.

CONGRESS of FREAKS at RINGLING BROTHERS and BARNUM & BAILEY (COMBINED) CIRCUS.

CENTURY

## CHAPTER IV

# THE CONGRESS OF FREAKS

Kelty's annual "class photograph" of the
sideshow exotics heralded the new season
of Ringling Brothers and Barnum & Bailey
Circus and were the most sought-after
of Kelty's images.

opposite: Congress of Freaks at Ringling Brothers and
Barnum & Bailey Circus, Madison Square Garden, 1924
right: Congress of Freaks at Ringling Brothers and
Barnum & Bailey Circus, Madison Square Garden, 1933 (detail)

Congress of Freaks at Ringling Brothers and Barnum & Bailey Circus, Madison Square Garden, 1925

CONGRESS OF FREAKS WITH RINGLING BROTHERS AND BARNUM & BAILEY COMBINED CIRCUS.
SEASON - 1927

Congress of Freaks at Ringling Brothers and Barnum & Bailey Circus, Madison Square Garden, 1927

Congress of Freaks at Ringling Brothers and Barnum & Bailey Circus, Madison Square Garden, 1928

Congress of Freaks at Ringling Brothers and Barnum & Bailey Circus, Madison Square Garden, 1933

CONGRESS of FREAKS with RINGLING BROTHERS and BARNUM & B

SEASON — 1929

Congress of Freaks at Ringling Brothers and Barnum & Bailey Circus, Madison Square Garden, 1929

109

"GARGANTUA THE GREAT"

PHILADELPHIA, PA.
MAY. 23RD 1938

RINGLING BROTHERS AND BARNUM & BAILEY COMBINED CIRCUS

PHOTO BY
E.J. KELTY
CENTURY
N.Y.C.

# CHAPTER V

# THE SUPPORT STAFF

## THEY MADE THE CIRCUS RUN

These were the unsung heros

who worked long hours

and often missed meals

to keep the circuses on the road.

Kelty photographed them all.

opposite: "Gargantua the Great," Ringling Brothers and
Barnum & Bailey Circus, Philadelphia, 1938
right: Ringling Brothers and Barnum & Bailey Circus staff,
Irvington, New Jersey, 1931 (detail)

Ringling Brothers and Barnum & Bailey
combined menagerie, Brooklyn, 1933

RNUM COOK HOUSE
JULY ———————— 1935
3URG , MASS.

Ringling Brothers and Barnum & Bailey
cookhouse, Fitchburg, Massachusetts, 1935

Ringling Brothers and Barnum & Bailey Circus baseball team, Manchester, New Hampshire, 1934

Circus wagon #102, the "Parade Wardrobe Tableau," carrying the Clown Band, Hagenbeck-Wallace Circus, Providence, Rhode Island, 1934

PHOTO BY
E.J.KELTY
CENTURY
74W47
N.Y.C.

RINGLING BROTHERS AND BARNUM & BAILEY
READING, PA.

CIRCUS TRAIN CREW.

JUNE 1 1934

Ringling Brothers and Barnum & Bailey Circus train crew,
Reading, Pennsylvania, 1934

SELLS FLOTO CIRCUS

SOUTH OZONE PARK, N.Y.
JUNE 6TH 1932

PHOTO BY
CENTURY
74 W 47TH ST.
N.Y.C.

Sells-Floto Circus, South Ozone Park, New York, 1932

GEORGE DENMAN AND HIS STAFF
IRVINGTON, N.J. —— JUNE 9TH 1931

George Denman and his staff, Ringling Brothers and Barnum & Bailey Circus, Irvington, New Jersey, 1931

Floyd Davidson and his tractor department, Ringling Brothers and
Barnum & Bailey Circus, Milwaukee, Wisconsin, 1936

DAVIDSON AND HIS TRACTOR DEPARTMENT
...G BROTHERS AND BARNUM & BAILEY CIRCUS

PHOTO BY
E.J. KELTY
CENTURY
110 W 46 N.Y.C.
31-B

Everette James and his band, Christy Brothers Circus, 1927

Candy butchers, Hagenbeck-Wallace Circus, Brooklyn, 1932

101 RANCH MIDWAY
NEWARK, N.J.
—1930—

## CHAPTER VI

# EXTERIOR AND INTERIOR VIEWS

Kelty's photographs of circus settings were just as important—and saleable— as his group shots and were popular with both fans and circuses alike.

opposite: 101 Ranch Midway, Newark, New Jersey, 1930
right: Hunt's Circus, Tarrytown, New York, 1933 (detail)

Silvan-Drew Motorized Circus, Mamaroneck, New York, 1929

Sam B. Dill's Circus, Mineola, New York, 1933

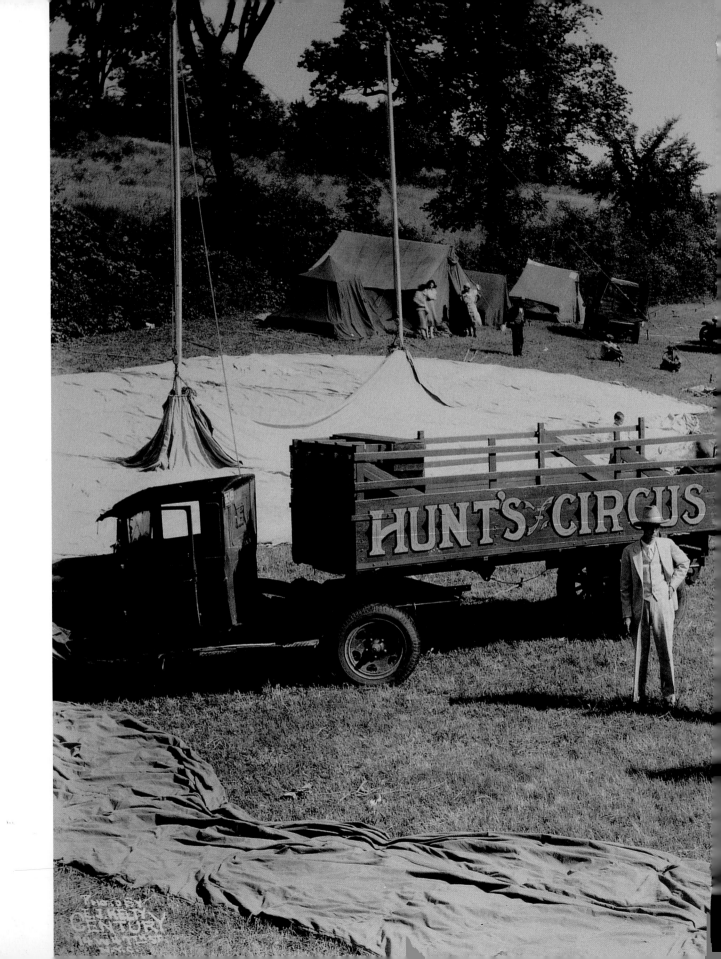

Hunt's Circus, Pawling, New York, 1933

PAWLING, N.Y. — JUNE 18TH 1933

PHOTO BY
E.J.KELTY
CENTURY
74 W 47TH ST.
N.Y.C.
2

Hunt's Circus, Tarrytown, New York, 1933

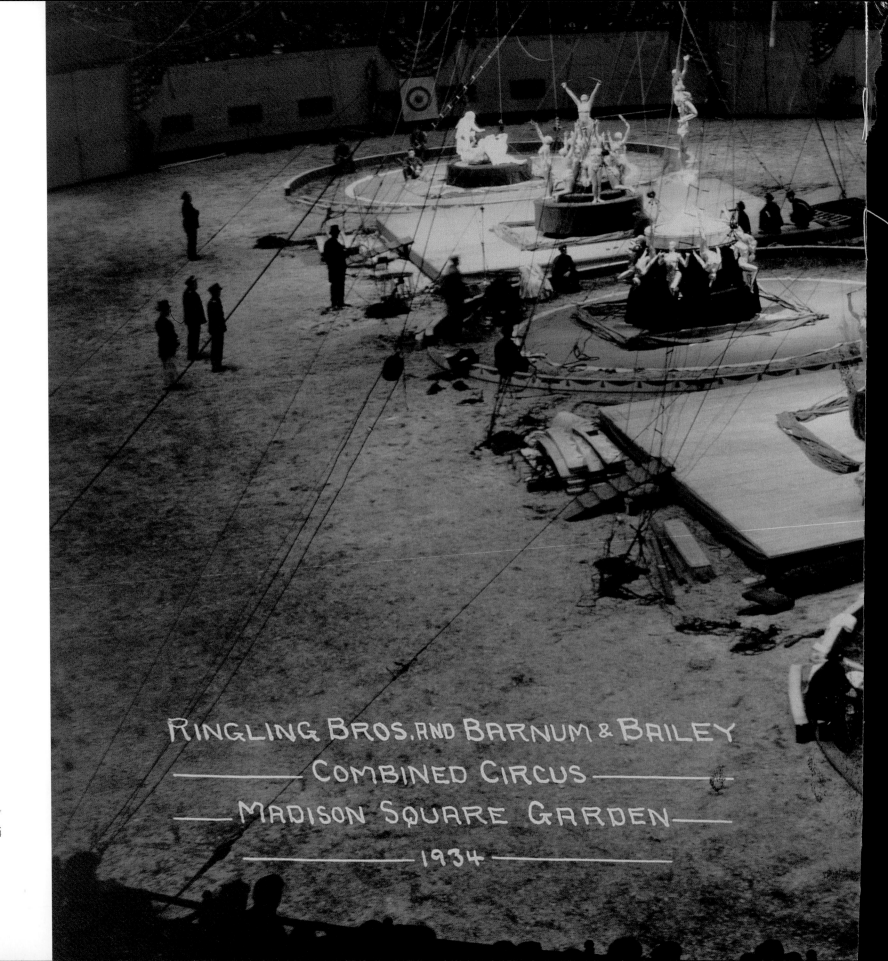

Ringling Brothers and Barnum & Bailey
Circus, Madison Square Garden, 1934

138

Photo By
CENTURY
74 W 47
N.Y.C.

Hagenbeck-Wallace Circus, Terra Haute, Indiana, 1934

E CIRCUS – TERRA HAUTE, INDIANA – MAY 17TH 1934

# APPENDIX

## NOTES ON THE PHOTOGRAPHS

Page 56: The WPA Circus was directed by Burns O'Sullivan and was part of the artists project of the Works Progress Administration. Many of the performers were retired or long past their prime, but some of the younger performers and actors, most notably Burt Lancaster, were just getting their start in show business. The WPA Circus was known mostly for its fifty-piece band and played primarily in and around New York City.

Page 62: Kelty's photograph of the Ringling Brothers and Barnum & Bailey Circus "Congress of Strange People—Combined Sideshows" hangs over the entrance to the sideshow tent.

Page 64: The Ringling Brothers purchased the Barnum & Bailey Circus in 1908. However, the circuses operated independently until 1919, when they merged. The term "combined" was used on all Ringling Brothers publicity from 1919 through the 1930s.

Page 74: The "Marcellus Golden Models" troupe performed with the Ringling Brothers and Barnum & Bailey Combined Circus in 1933 and 1934. In 1933, they were listed as acrobats and as doing aerial ballet, flying ballet plastique, a statuary act, and a posing act. In 1934, the troupe (billed as "9 girls, one male") performed as acrobats, statuary (as "Golden Models"), "Living Art in Bronze," a posing act, and in aerial ballet.

Page 83: Born Frederick Ferber, Fred Bradna assumed the last name of his wife, Ella. Ella Bradna was a star equestrian in the center ring of Ringling Brothers and Barnum & Bailey Circus for twenty-nine consecutive seasons.

Pages 84–85 and 87: Famous animal tamer Clyde Beatty made his reputation by working alone in a cage surrounded by as many as forty lions and tigers.

Page 86: Tom Mix was considered one of the biggest stars of silent western films. In 1929, Mix concluded his silent film career and became the headliner for Sells-Floto Circus between 1929 and 1931.

Page 88: In 1931, the equestrian Hanneford family performed with both the Hagenbeck-Wallace and the Sells-Floto circuses. Edwin "Poodles" Hanneford is shown in the long fur coat he wore during his comedy-riding act. Left to right: Percy Clark, Mrs. Poodles Hanneford, Poodles, Mrs. Hanneford (Poodles' mother), Mrs. Ernie Clark, and Ernie Clark.

Pages 92–93: Harold Barnes (on the wire above the girls' heads) was a high-wire artist for Cole Bros. Circus during the 1935, 1936, and 1937 seasons. In 2001, he wrote the following in a letter to Miles Barth: "I remember Edward Kelty well, he was known as 'the circus photographer.'"

I joined Cole Bros., when I was fourteen years old and featured just under Clyde Beatty, the famous wild animal trainer. Kelty took two [photographs] of the same layout, one was where I was in a split and another, crouching down. The girls under the wire were actually used in a performance in an opening created by the producer, Rex de Roselli. Since I was so young, he wanted a number simulating a college or high school. So he gave the girls tennis racquets and me a ukulele and we ran out into the center ring and did a short dance to the song "I Got Rhythm." At the end of the dance the girls lined up behind me under the wire and the announcer announced the act. I handed the 'uke' to the girl on the end and climbed up on the pedestal for the performance. The circus used the crouching pose for advertising billing and one would find the photograph on billboards and barns throughout the country."

Pages 94-95: The Knight Troupe was made up of wirewalkers and teeterboard artists. The words "Rush Proof" would be stamped onto quick-processed prints of the favorite image from the photography session. These proofs were then given to the client for approval so final prints could be made. On this particular image, Kelty wrote his prices for prints being ordered.

Page 105: For the opening of the 1927 season, Clyde Ingalls, the manager of the sideshow for Ringling Brothers and Barnum & Bailey Circus, advertised the following exhibits: Tom Ton, fat boy; Haig, the elastic skin man; Adrienne, the bearded lady; Ho Jo, the bear boy; Baron Paucci, midget; Slats, skeleton sheik; Anderson Sisters, spotted girls; Mlle. Cleo, snake charmer; Eko and Iko, "ambassadors from Mars"; Fairy Airy Lillian Maloney, albino; The Dancing Dolls; Jim Tarver, giant; Carlson Sisters, boxing fat girls; Olga, bearded lady; Freddy, the armless wonder; Major Mite, the smallest man on earth; Jack Earle, Texas giant; Professor Henri, India-rubber man; Miss Katie, armless wonder; Jolly Irene, fat girl; Baby Doll, fat girl; Twisto, the human knot; Miss Artorio, the tattooed wonder; Miss Pictorio, tattooed girl; Ima Whale, fat girl; Peter Robinson, skeleton man; Ajax, The Sword Swallower; Koo Koo, the bird girl; Baby Bunny, fat girl; Miss Dend, sword swallower; Clicko, African Bushman; and Roy Eddy Clark's collection of reptiles.

Page 119: A number of the larger circuses had baseball teams. They would usually play local teams or teams from other circuses and were made up of both performers and circus personnel.

# ILLUSTRATION AND PHOTOGRAPH CREDITS

All photographs © Edward J. Kelty, except page 2 © Eddie Jackson; pages 12, 15, and 19 photographer unknown; and page 20 © Harry Atwell

Endpapers, front and back: Alan Siegel Collection
Page 2: The Pfening Collection
Page 5: Ken Harck Collection

## PREFACE
Pages 6–7 and 9: Alan Siegel Collection
Page 11: The Pfening Collection

## EDWARD J. KELTY AND CENTURY FLASHLIGHT PHOTOGRAPHERS
Pages 12, 15, 16, 17, and 19: The Pfening Collection

## THE MAGIC CALVALCADE
Page 20: Harry Atwell photograph, Circus World Museum, Baraboo, Wisconsin
Pages 22, 23, and 24: The Pfening Collection
Page 26: Ken Harck Collection
Page 27 (right): The Pfening Collection
Page 27 (left): Tibbals-Dunn Collection
Page 28: The Pfening Collection
Page 30: Circus World Museum, Baraboo, Wisconsin
Pages 31, 32, and 33: The Pfening Collection

## CHAPTER I
Page 36: Ken Harck Collection
Page 37: Tibbals-Dunn Collection
Pages 38 and 39: Ken Harck Collection
Pages 40–41: The Pfening Collection

Pages 42: Ken Harck Collection
Pages 43 and 44: Tibbals-Dunn Collection
Pages 46–47: Ken Harck Collection
Page 48: Alan Siegel Collection
Pages 49, 50, 51, and 52: Ken Harck Collection
Page 53: Tibbals-Dunn Collection
Page 54: Ken Harck Collection

## CHAPTER II
Pages 56 and 57: Alan Siegel Collection
Pages 58–59: The Pfening Collection
Page 60: Ken Harck Collection
Page 61: The Pfening Collection
Pages 62 and 63: Ken Harck Collection
Page 64: Alan Siegel Collection
Pages 65, 66–67, and 68: Alan Siegel Collection
Pages 69 and 70: The Pfening Collection
Page 71: Ken Harck Collection
Page 72: Tibbals-Dunn Collection
Page 73: Ken Harck Collection

## CHAPTER III
Page 74: Alan Siegel Collection
Page 75: Tibbals-Dunn Collection
Pages 76–77: Alan Siegel Collection
Page 79: The Pfening Collection
Pages 81 and 82: Tibbals-Dunn Collection
Page 83: The Pfening Collection
Pages 84–85: Alan Siegel Collection
Pages 86 and 87: Tibbals-Dunn Collection
Page 88: Alan Siegel Collection

Pages 89, 90–91, 92–93, 94, and 95: Tibbals-Dunn Collection
Pages 96–97: The Pfening Collection
Pages 98, 99, and 101: Alan Siegel Collection

## CHAPTER IV
Page 102: Tibbals-Dunn Collection
Page 103: Alan Siegel Collection
Pages 104 and 105: Tibbals-Dunn Collection
Page 106: Ken Harck Collection
Page 107: The Pfening Collection
Pages 108–109: Alan Siegel Collection

## CHAPTER V
Page 110: Circus World Museum, Baraboo, Wisconsin
Pages 111, 112–113, and 114: Alan Siegel Collection
Page 115: The Pfening Collection
Pages 116–117 and 119: Tibbals-Dunn Collection
Pages 120, 121, 122–123, and 124: The Pfening Collection
Page 125: Alan Siegel Collection
Pages 126–127: Ken Harck Collection
Page 128: Tibbals-Dunn Collection
Page 129: Tibbals-Dunn Collection

## CHAPTER VI
Pages 130, 131, and 132: The Pfening Collection
Page 133: Alan Siegel Collection
Pages 134–135, 136–137, and 138–139: The Pfening Collection
Pages 140–141: Alan Siegel Collection

SELLS-FLOTO CIRCUS
ZACK TERRELL, MANAGER
— FRED LEDGETT —
EQUESTRIAN DIRECTOR

Clowns celebrating the "Ringling Golden Jubilee," Brooklyn, 1933

Clowns, Hagenbeck-Wallace Circus, c. 1935

Hagenbeck-Wallace Circus performers, Bronx, New York, 1933

John Robinson Circus clowns, Schenectady, New York, 1928

Gangler's Novelty Circus, New York, c. 1931

"MARCELLUS GOLDEN MODELS"

## CHAPTER III

# SOLO, INDEPENDENT, AND GROUP PERFORMERS

Performers from some of the greatest
circus acts of the 1920s and 1930s
posed for Kelty during his career.

opposite: Marcellus Golden Models, 1933
right: Harold Barnes, Clyde Beatty–Cole Bros. Circus, Little Falls, New York, 1935

Hugo Zacchini, Human Projectile, Ringling Brothers and Barnum & Bailey Circus, Brooklyn, 1933

HUGO ZACCHINI — HUMAN PROJECTILE
RINGLING BROTHERS AND BARNUM & BAILEY COMBINED CIRCUS

PHOTO BY
E.J. KELTY
CENTURY
74 W 45TH ST.
N.Y.C.

Dorothy Herbert, Ringling Brothers and Barnum & Bailey Circus, c. 1935

Cheerful Gardner, Hagenbeck-Wallace Circus, c. 1933

CHEERFUL GARDNER

WAGENBECK-WALLACE CIRCUS

Col. Tom Carver, Tom Ton, and Major Mite, Ringling Brothers and Barnum & Bailey Circus, Madison Square Garden, 1924

Fred Bradna, Equestrian Director, Ringling Brothers and Barnum & Bailey Circus, Madison Square Garden, 1930